Fresh Strawberry Sponge Cake

INGREDIENTS

Serves 8–10

175 g/6 oz unsalted
   butter, softened
175 g/6 oz caster sugar
1 tsp vanilla essence
3 large eggs, beaten
175 g/6 oz self-raising flour
150 ml/¼ pint double cream
2 tbsp icing sugar, sifted
225 g/8 oz fresh strawberries, hulled
   and chopped
few extra strawberries, to decorate

HELPFUL HINT

For sponge cakes, it is important to achieve the correct consistency of the uncooked mixture. Check it after folding in the flour by tapping a spoonful of the mixture on the side of the bowl. If it drops easily, 'dropping' consistency has been reached. If it is too stiff, fold in a tablespoon of cooled boiled water.

1 Preheat the oven to 190°C/375°F/Gas Mark 5, 10 minutes before baking. Lightly oil and line the bases of 2 x 20.5 cm/8 inch round cake tins with greaseproof or baking paper.

2 Using an electric whisk, beat the butter, sugar and vanilla essence until pale and fluffy. Gradually beat in the eggs a little at a time, beating well between each addition.

3 Sift half the flour over the mixture and using a metal spoon or rubber spatula gently fold into the mixture. Sift over the remaining flour and fold in until just blended.

4 Divide the mixture between the tins, spreading evenly. Gently smooth the surfaces with the back of a spoon. Bake in the centre of the preheated oven for 20–25 minutes, or until well risen and golden.

5 Remove and leave to cool before turning out on to a wire rack. Whip the cream with 1 tablespoon of the icing sugar until it forms soft peaks. Fold in the chopped strawberries.

6 Spread 1 cake layer evenly with the mixture and top with the second cake layer, rounded side up.

7 Thickly dust the cake with icing sugar and decorate with the reserved strawberries. Carefully slide on to a serving plate and serve.

2

4

6

Almond Angel Cake with Amaretto Cream

INGREDIENTS

Cuts into 10–12 slices

175 g/6 oz icing sugar, plus
  2–3 tbsp
150 g/5 oz plain flour
350 ml/12 fl oz egg whites (about 10
  large egg whites)
1½ tsp cream of tartar
½ tsp vanilla essence
1 tsp almond essence
¼ tsp salt
200 g/7 oz caster sugar
175 ml/6 fl oz double cream
2 tablespoons Amaretto liqueur
fresh raspberries, to decorate

FOOD FACT

Angel cake has a very light and delicate texture, and can be difficult to slice. For best results, use 2 forks gently to separate a portion of the cake.

1 Preheat the oven to 180°C/350°F/Gas Mark 4, 10 minutes before baking. Sift together the 175 g/6 oz icing sugar and flour. Stir to blend, then sift again and reserve.

2 Using an electric whisk, beat the egg whites, cream of tartar, vanilla essence, ½ teaspoon of almond essence and salt on medium speed until soft peaks form. Gradually add the caster sugar, 2 tablespoons at a time, beating well after each addition, until stiff peaks form.

3 Sift about one-third of the flour mixture over the egg white mixture and using a metal spoon or rubber spatula, gently fold into the egg white mixture. Repeat, folding the flour mixture into the egg white mixture in 2 more batches. Spoon gently into an ungreased angel food cake tin or 25.5 cm/10 inch tube tin.

4 Bake in the preheated oven until risen and golden on top and the surface springs back quickly when gently pressed with a clean finger. Immediately invert the cake tin and cool completely in the tin.

5 When cool, carefully run a sharp knife around the edge of the tin and the centre ring to loosen the cake from the edge. Using the fingertips, ease the cake from the tin and invert on to a cake plate. Thickly dust the cake with the extra icing sugar.

6 Whip the cream with the remaining almond essence, Amaretto liqueur and a little more icing sugar, until soft peaks form.

7 Fill a piping bag fitted with a star nozzle with half the cream and pipe around the bottom edge of the cake. Decorate the edge with the fresh raspberries and serve the remaining cream separately.

1

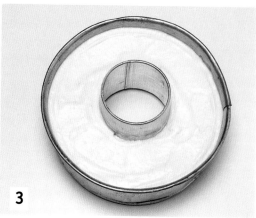

3

7

Luxury Carrot Cake

INGREDIENTS

Cuts into 12 slices

275 g/10 oz plain flour
2 tsp baking powder
1 tsp bicarbonate of soda
1 tsp salt
2 tsp ground cinnamon
1 tsp ground ginger
200 g/7 oz dark soft brown sugar
100 g/3½ oz caster sugar
4 large eggs, beaten
250 ml/9 fl oz sunflower oil
1 tbsp vanilla essence
4 carrots, peeled and shredded
   (about 450 g/1 lb)
380 g/14 oz can crushed pineapple,
   well drained
125 g/4 oz pecans or walnuts, toasted
   and chopped

For the frosting:
175 g/6 oz cream cheese, softened
50 g/2 oz butter, softened
1 tsp vanilla essence
225 g/8 oz icing sugar, sifted
1–2 tbsp milk

1 Preheat the oven to 180°C/350°F/Gas Mark 4, 10 minutes before baking. Lightly oil a 33 x 23 cm/13 x 9 inch baking tin. Line the base with non-stick baking paper, oil and dust with flour.

2 Sift the first 6 ingredients into a large bowl and stir in the sugars to blend. Make a well in the centre.

3 Beat the eggs, oil and vanilla essence together and pour into the well. Using an electric whisk, gradually beat, drawing in the flour mixture from the side until a smooth batter forms. Stir in the carrots, crushed pineapple and chopped nuts until blended.

4 Pour into the prepared tin and smooth the surface evenly. Bake in the preheated oven for 50 minutes, or until firm and a skewer inserted into the centre comes out clean. Remove from the oven and leave to cool before removing from the tin and discarding the lining paper.

5 For the frosting, beat the cream cheese, butter and vanilla essence together until smooth, then gradually beat in the icing sugar until the frosting is smooth. Add a little milk, if necessary. Spread the frosting over the top. Refrigerate for about 1 hour to set the frosting, then cut into squares and serve.

2

3

5

White Chocolate Cheesecake

INGREDIENTS

Cuts into 16 slices

For the base:
150 g/5 oz digestive biscuits
50 g/2 oz whole almonds,
 lightly toasted
50 g/2 oz butter, melted
½ tsp almond essence

For the filling:
350 g/12 oz good-quality white
 chocolate, chopped
125 ml/4 fl oz double cream
700 g/1½ lb cream
 cheese, softened
50 g/2 oz caster sugar
4 large eggs
2 tbsp Amaretto or
 almond-flavour liqueur

For the topping:
450 ml/¾ pint soured cream
50 g/2 oz caster sugar
½ tsp almond or vanilla essence
white chocolate curls,
 to decorate

1 Preheat the oven to 180°C/350°F/Gas Mark 4, 10 minutes before baking. Lightly oil a 23 x 7.5 cm/9 x 3 inch springform tin. Crush the biscuits and almonds in a food processor to form fine crumbs. Pour in the butter and almond essence and blend. Pour the crumbs into the tin and using the back of a spoon, press on to the bottom and up the sides to within 1 cm/½ inch of the top of the tin edge.

2 Bake in the preheated oven for 5 minutes to set. Remove and transfer to a wire rack. Reduce the oven temperature to 150°C/300°F/Gas Mark 2.

3 Heat the white chocolate and cream in a saucepan over a low heat, stirring constantly until melted. Remove and cool.

4 Beat the cream cheese and sugar until smooth. Add the eggs, one at a time, beating well after each addition. Slowly beat in the cooled white chocolate cream and the Amaretto and pour into the baked crust. Place on a baking tray and bake for 45–55 minutes, until the edge of the cake is firm, but the centre is slightly soft. Reduce the oven temperature if the top begins to brown. Remove to a wire rack and increase the temperature to 200°C/400°F/Gas Mark 6.

5 To make the topping, beat the soured cream, sugar and almond or vanilla essence until smooth and gently pour over the cheesecake, tilting the pan to distribute the topping evenly. Alternatively spread with a metal palette knife.

6 Bake for another 5 minutes to set. Turn off the oven and leave the door halfway open for about 1 hour. Transfer to a wire rack and run a sharp knife around the edge of the crust to separate from the tin. Cool and refrigerate until chilled. Remove from the tin, decorate with white chocolate curls and serve.

1

4

5

Rich Devil's Food Cake

INGREDIENTS

Cuts into 12–16 slices

450 g/1 lb plain flour
1 tbsp bicarbonate of soda
½ tsp salt
75 g/3 oz cocoa powder
300 ml/½ pint milk
150 g/5 oz butter, softened
400 g/14 oz soft dark brown sugar
2 tsp vanilla essence
4 large eggs

For the chocolate fudge frosting:

275 g/10 oz caster sugar
½ tsp salt
125 g/4 oz plain dark
  chocolate, chopped
225 ml/8 fl oz milk
2 tbsp golden syrup
125 g/4 oz butter, diced
2 tsp vanilla essence

1 Preheat the oven to 180°C/350°F/Gas Mark 4, 10 minutes before baking. Lightly oil and line the bases of 3 x 23 cm/9 inch cake tins with greaseproof or baking paper. Sift the flour, bicarbonate of soda and salt into a bowl.

2 Sift the cocoa powder into another bowl and gradually whisk in a little of the milk to form a paste. Continue whisking in the milk until a smooth mixture results.

3 Beat the butter, sugar and vanilla essence until light and fluffy then gradually beat in the eggs, beating well after each addition. Stir in the flour and cocoa mixtures alternately in 3 or 4 batches.

4 Divide the mixture evenly among the 3 tins, smoothing the surfaces evenly. Bake in the preheated oven for 25–35 minutes, until cooked and firm to the touch. Remove, cool and turn out on to a wire rack. Discard the lining paper.

5 To make the frosting, put the sugar, salt and chocolate into a heavy based saucepan and stir in the milk until blended. Add the golden syrup and butter. Bring the mixture to the boil over a medium-high heat, stirring to help dissolve the sugar.

6 Boil for 1 minute, stirring constantly. Remove from the heat, stir in the vanilla essence and cool. When cool, whisk until thickened and slightly lightened in colour.

7 Sandwich the 3 cake layers together with about a third of the frosting, placing the third cake layer with the flat side up. Transfer the cake to a serving plate and, using a metal palette knife, spread the remaining frosting over the top and sides. Swirl the top to create a decorative effect and serve.

2

5

7

Coffee & Walnut Gateau with Brandied Prunes

INGREDIENTS

Cuts into 10–12 slices

For the prunes:
225 g/8 oz ready-to-eat pitted
   dried prunes
150 ml/¼ pint cold tea
3 tbsp brandy

For the cake:
450 g/1 lb walnut pieces
50 g/2 oz self-raising flour
½ tsp baking powder
1 tsp instant coffee powder
   (not granules)
5 large eggs, separated
¼ tsp cream of tartar
150 g/5 oz caster sugar
2 tbsp sunflower oil
8 walnut halves, to decorate

For the filling:
600 ml/1 pint double cream
4 tbsp icing sugar, sifted
2 tbsp coffee-flavoured liqueur

1. Preheat the oven to 180°C/350°F/Gas Mark 4, 10 minutes before baking. Put the prunes in a small bowl with the tea and brandy and allow to stand for 3–4 hours or overnight. Oil and line the bases of 2 x 23 cm/ 9 inch cake tins. Chop the walnut pieces in a food processor. Reserve a quarter of the nuts. Add the flour, baking powder and coffee and blend until finely ground.

2. Whisk the egg whites with the cream of tartar until soft peaks form. Sprinkle in one-third of the sugar, 2 tablespoons at a time, until stiff peaks form. In another bowl, beat the egg yolks, oil and the remaining sugar, until thick. Using a metal spoon or rubber spatula, alternately fold in the nut mixture and egg whites until just blended.

3. Divide the mixture evenly between the tins, smoothing the tops. Bake in the preheated oven for 30–35 minutes, or until the top of the cakes spring back when lightly pressed with a clean finger. Remove from the oven and cool. Remove from the tins and discard the lining paper.

4. Drain the prunes, reserving the soaking liquid. Dry on kitchen paper, then chop and reserve. Whisk the cream with the icing sugar and liqueur until soft peaks form. Spoon one-eighth of the cream into a pastry bag fitted with a star nozzle.

5. Cut the cake layers in half horizontally. Sprinkle each cut side with 1 tablespoon of the reserved prune-soaking liquid. Sandwich the cakes together with half of the cream and all of the chopped prunes.

6. Spread the remaining cream around the sides of the cake and press in the reserved chopped walnuts. Pipe rosettes around the edge of the cake. Decorate with walnut halves and serve.

1

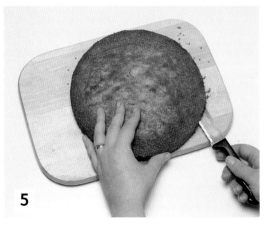

5

6

Wild Strawberry & Rose Petal Jam Cake

INGREDIENTS

Cuts into 8 servings

275 g/10 oz plain flour

1 tsp baking powder

¼ tsp salt

150 g/5 oz unsalted
  butter, softened

200 g/7 oz caster sugar

2 large eggs, beaten

2 tbsp rosewater

125 ml/4 fl oz milk

125 g/4 oz rose petal or strawberry
  jam, slightly warmed

125 g/4 oz wild strawberries, hulled,
  or baby strawberries, chopped

frosted rose petals, to decorate

For the rose cream filling:

200 ml/7 fl oz double cream

25 ml/1 fl oz natural
  Greek yogurt

2 tbsp rosewater

1–2 tbsp icing sugar

1 Preheat the oven to 180°C/350°F/Gas Mark 4, 10 minutes before baking. Lightly oil and flour a 20.5 cm/8 inch non-stick cake tin. Sift the flour, baking powder and salt into a bowl and reserve.

2 Beat the butter and sugar until light and fluffy. Beat in the eggs, a little at a time, then stir in the rosewater. Gently fold in the flour mixture and milk with a metal spoon or rubber spatula and mix lightly together.

3 Spoon the cake mixture into the tin, spreading evenly and smoothing the top.

4 Bake in the preheated oven for 25–30 minutes, or until well risen and golden and the centre springs back when pressed with a clean finger. Remove and cool, then remove from the tin.

5 For the filling, whisk the cream, yogurt, 1 tablespoon of rosewater and 1 tablespoon of icing sugar until soft peaks form. Split the cake horizontally in half and sprinkle with the remaining rosewater.

6 Spread the warmed jam on the base of the cake. Top with half the whipped cream mixture, then sprinkle with half the strawberries. Place the remaining cake half on top. Spread with the remaining cream and swirl, if desired. Decorate with the rose petals. Dust the cake lightly with a little icing sugar and serve.

2

5

6

Chocolate Mousse Cake

INGREDIENTS

Serves 8–10

For the cake:
450 g/1 lb plain dark
   chocolate, chopped
125 g/4 oz butter, softened
3 tbsp brandy
9 large eggs, separated
150 g/5 oz caster sugar

For the chocolate glaze:
225 ml/8 fl oz double cream
225 g/8 oz plain dark
   chocolate, chopped
2 tbsp brandy
1 tbsp single cream and white
   chocolate curls, to decorate

FOOD FACT
Wonderfully rich and delicious served with a fruity compote – why not try making cherry compote using either fresh, if in season, or otherwise tinned in fruit juice. Stone the cherries, or drain and then simmer on a low heat with a little apple juice until reduced.

1 Preheat the oven to 180°C/350°F/Gas Mark 4, 10 minutes before baking. Lightly oil and line the bases of 2 x 20.5 cm/8 inch springform tins with baking paper. Melt the chocolate and butter in a bowl set over a saucepan of simmering water. Stir until smooth. Remove from the heat and stir in the brandy.

2 Whisk the egg yolks and the sugar, reserving 2 tablespoons of the sugar, until thick and creamy. Slowly beat in the chocolate mixture until smooth and well blended. Whisk the egg whites until soft peaks form, then sprinkle over the remaining sugar and continue whisking until stiff but not dry.

3 Gently fold the egg whites into the chocolate mixture. Divide about two-thirds of the mixture evenly between the tins, tapping to distribute the mixture evenly. Reserve the remaining one-third of the chocolate mousse mixture for the filling. Bake in the preheated oven for about 20 minutes, or until the cakes are well risen and set. Remove and cool for at least 1 hour.

4 Loosen the edges of the cake layers with a knife. Using the fingertips, lightly press the crusty edges down. Pour the rest of the mousse over one layer, spreading until even. Carefully unclip the side, remove the other cake from the tin and gently invert on to the mousse, bottom side up to make a flat top layer. Discard lining paper and chill for 4–6 hours, or until set.

5 To make the glaze, melt the cream and chocolate with the brandy in a heavy based saucepan and stir until smooth. Cool until thickened. Unclip the side of the mousse cake and place on a wire rack. Pour over half the glaze and spread to cover. Allow to set, then decorate with chocolate curls. To serve, heat the remaining glaze and pour round each slice, and dot with cream.

1

2

4

Christmas Cake

INGREDIENTS

Cuts into 12–18 slices

900 g/2 lb mixed dried fruit

75 g/3 oz glacé cherries, rinsed
and halved

3 tbsp brandy or orange juice

finely grated zest and juice of 1 lemon

225 g/8 oz soft dark muscovado sugar

225 g/8 oz butter, at room
temperature

4 medium eggs, beaten

225 g/8 oz plain flour

1 tbsp black treacle

1 tbsp mixed spice

To decorate:

2–4 tbsp brandy (optional)

4 tbsp sieved apricot jam

700 g/1½ lb almond paste (see
page 46)

icing sugar, for dusting

1 kg/2 lb 3 oz ready-to-roll sugarpaste

bought decorations and ribbon

1 Place the dried fruit and cherries in a bowl and sprinkle over the brandy or orange juice and the lemon zest and juice. Stir and let soak for 2–4 hours. Preheat the oven to 150°C/300°F/Gas Mark 2. Grease and double-line the base and sides of a 20.5 cm/8 inch round deep cake tin.

2 Beat the sugar and butter together until soft and fluffy. Beat the eggs in gradually, adding 1 teaspoon of flour with each addition. Stir in the treacle, then sift in the rest of the flour and the spice. Add the soaked fruit and stir until the mixture is smooth.

3 Spoon into the tin and smooth the top level. Bake for 1 hour, then reduce the temperature to 140°C/275°F/Gas Mark 1 and bake for a further 2–2½ hours until a skewer inserted into the centre comes out clean. Leave the cake to cool in the tin, then, when completely cold, remove and wrap in greaseproof paper and then in foil and store in a cool place for 1–3 months.

4 To decorate, brush the cake all over with brandy, if using. Heat the jam and brush over the top and sides. Roll out one third of the almond paste and cut into a disc the size of the top of the cake, using the empty tin as a guide. Place the disc on top. Roll the remaining paste into a strip long enough to cover the sides of the cake and press on. Leave the marzipan to dry out in a cool place for 2 days.

5 On a surface dusted with icing sugar, roll out the sugarpaste to a circle large enough to cover the top and sides of the cake. Brush 1 tablespoon brandy or cold boiled water over the almond paste and place the sugarpaste on top. Smooth down and trim. Make a border from tiny balls of sugarpaste and decorate.

3

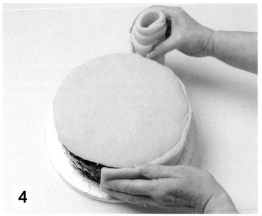

4

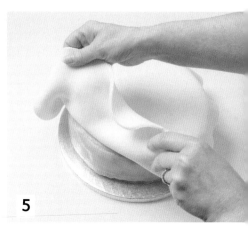

5

Christmas Cranberry Chocolate Roulade

INGREDIENTS

Cuts into 12–14 slices

For the chocolate ganache frosting:
300 ml/½ pint double cream

350 g/12 oz plain dark
 chocolate, chopped

2 tbsp brandy (optional)

For the roulade:
5 large eggs, separated

3 tbsp cocoa powder, sifted, plus
 extra for dusting

125 g/4 oz icing sugar, sifted, plus
 extra for dusting

¼ tsp cream of tartar

For the filling:
175 g/6 oz cranberry sauce

½ tbsp brandy (optional)

450 ml/¾ pint double cream,
 whipped to soft peaks

To decorate:
caramelised orange strips

dried cranberries

1 Preheat the oven to 200°C /400°F/Gas Mark 6. Bring the cream to the boil over a medium heat. Remove from the heat and add all of the chocolate, stirring until melted. Stir in the brandy, if using and strain into a medium bowl. Cool, then refrigerate for 6–8 hours.

2 Lightly oil and line a 39 x 26 cm/15 ½ x 10½ inch Swiss roll tin with non-stick baking paper. Using an electric whisk, beat the egg yolks until thick and creamy. Slowly beat in the cocoa powder and half the icing sugar and reserve. Whisk the egg whites and cream of tartar into soft peaks. Gradually whisk in the remaining sugar until the mixture is stiff and glossy. Gently fold the yolk mixture into the egg whites with a metal spoon or rubber spatula. Spread evenly into the tin.

3 Bake in the preheated oven for 15 minutes. Remove and invert on to a large sheet of greaseproof paper, dusted with cocoa powder. Cut off the crisp edges of the cake then roll up. Leave on a wire rack until cold.

4 For the filling, heat the cranberry sauce with the brandy, if using, until warm and spreadable. Unroll the cooled cake and spread with the cranberry sauce. Allow to cool and set. Carefully spoon the whipped cream over the surface and spread to within 2.5 cm/1 inch of the edges. Re-roll the cake. Transfer to a cake plate or tray.

5 Allow the chocolate ganache to soften at room temperature, then beat until soft and of a spreadable consistency. Spread over the roulade and, using a fork, mark the roulade with ridges to resemble tree bark. Dust with icing sugar. Decorate with the caramelised orange strips and dried cranberries and serve.

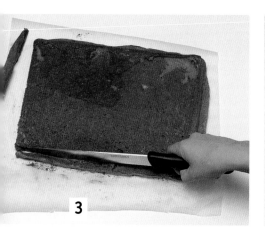

3

4

5

Celebration Fruit Cake

INGREDIENTS

Cuts into 16 slices

125 g/4 oz butter or margarine
125 g/4 oz soft dark brown sugar
380 g can crushed pineapple
150 g/5 oz raisins
150 g/5 oz sultanas
125 g/4 oz crystallised ginger,
  finely chopped
125 g/4 oz glacé cherries,
  coarsely chopped
125 g/4 oz mixed cut peel
225 g/8 oz self-raising flour
1 tsp bicarbonate of soda
2 tsp mixed spice
1 tsp ground cinnamon
$\frac{1}{2}$ tsp salt
2 large eggs, beaten

For the topping:

100 g/3$\frac{1}{2}$ oz pecan or walnut halves,
  lightly toasted
125 g/4 oz red, green and yellow
  glacé cherries
100 g/3$\frac{1}{2}$ oz small pitted prunes
  or dates
2 tbsp clear honey

1 Preheat the oven to 170°C/325°F/Gas Mark 3, 10 minutes before baking. Heat the butter and sugar in a saucepan until the sugar has dissolved, stirring frequently.

2 Add the pineapple and juice, dried fruits and peel. Bring to the boil, simmer 3 minutes, stirring occasionally, the remove from the heat to cool completely.

3 Lightly oil and line the base of a 20.5 x 7.5 cm/8 x 3 inch loose-bottomed cake tin with non-stick baking paper. Sift the flour, bicarbonate of soda, spices and salt into a bowl.

4 Add the boiled fruit mixture to the flour with the eggs and mix. Spoon into the tin and smooth the top. Bake in the preheated oven for 1¼ hours, or until a skewer inserted into the centre comes out clean. (If the cake is browning too quickly, cover loosely with tinfoil and reduce the oven temperature.)

5 Remove and cool completely before removing from the tin and discarding the lining paper.

6 Arrange the nuts, cherries and prunes or dates in an attractive pattern on top of the cake. Heat the honey and brush over the topping to glaze.

7 Alternatively, toss the nuts and fruits in the warm honey and spread evenly over the top of the cake. Cool completely and store in a cake tin for a day or two before serving to allow the flavours to develop.

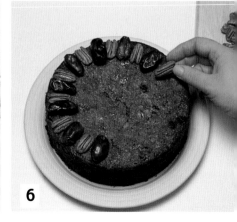

Orange Fruit Cake

INGREDIENTS

Cuts into 10–12 slices

For the orange cake:

225 g/8 oz self-raising flour
2 tsp baking powder
225 g/8 oz caster sugar
225 g/8 oz butter, softened
4 large eggs
grated zest of 1 orange
2 tbsp orange juice
2–3 tbsp Cointreau
125 g/4 oz chopped nuts
Cape gooseberries, blueberries,
  raspberries and mint sprigs
  to decorate
icing sugar, to dust (optional)

For the filling:

450 ml/³⁄₄ pint double cream
50 ml/2 fl oz Greek yogurt
¹⁄₂ tsp vanilla essence
2–3 tbsp Cointreau
1 tbsp icing sugar
450 g/1 lb orange fruits, such as
  mango, peach, nectarine, papaya
  and yellow plums

1 Preheat the oven to 180°C/350°F/Gas Mark 4, 10 minutes before baking. Lightly oil and line the base of a 25.5 cm/10 inch ring mould tin or deep springform tin with non-stick baking paper.

2 Sift the flour and baking powder into a large bowl and stir in the sugar. Make a well in the centre and add the butter, eggs, grated zest and orange juice. Beat until blended and a smooth batter is formed. Turn into the tin and smooth the top.

3 Bake in the preheated oven for 35–45 minutes, or until golden and the sides begin to shrink from the edge of the tin. Remove, cool before removing from the tin and discard the lining paper.

4 Using a serrated knife, cut the cake horizontally about one-third from the top and remove the top layer of the cake. If not using a ring mould tin, scoop out a centre ring of sponge from the top third and the bottom two-thirds of the layer, making a hollow tunnel. Reserve for a trifle or other dessert. Sprinkle the cut sides with the Cointreau.

5 For the filling, whip the cream and yogurt with the vanilla essence, Cointreau and icing sugar until soft peaks form.

6 Chop the orange fruits and fold into the cream. Spoon some of this mixture on to the bottom cake layer, mounding it slightly. Transfer to a serving plate.

7 Cover with the top layer of sponge and spread the remaining cream mixture over the top and sides.

8 Press the chopped nuts into the sides of the cake and decorate the top with the Cape gooseberries, blueberries and raspberries. If liked, dust the top with icing sugar and serve.

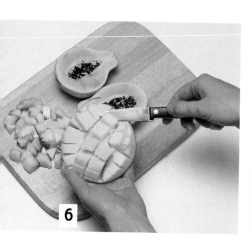

6

7

8

Chocolate Box Cake

INGREDIENTS

Cuts into 16 slices

For the chocolate sponge:

175 g/6 oz self-raising flour

1 tsp baking powder

175 g/6 oz caster sugar

175 g/6 oz butter, softened

3 large eggs

25 g/1 oz cocoa powder

150 g/5 oz apricot preserve

cocoa powder, to dust

For the chocolate box:

275 g/10 oz plain dark chocolate

For the topping:

450 ml/³/₄ pint double cream

275 g/10 oz plain dark
  chocolate, melted

2 tbsp brandy

1 tsp cocoa powder to decorate

1 Preheat the oven to 180°C/350°F/Gas Mark 4, 10 minutes before baking. Lightly oil and flour a 20.5 cm/8 inch square cake tin. Sift the flour and baking powder into a large bowl and stir in the sugar.

2 Using an electric whisk, beat in the butter and eggs. Blend the cocoa powder with 1 tablespoon of water, then beat into the creamed mixture. Turn into the tin and bake in the preheated oven for about 25 minutes, or until well risen and cooked. Remove and cool before removing the cake from the tin.

3 To make the chocolate box, break the chocolate into small pieces, place in a heatproof bowl over a saucepan of gently simmering water and leave until soft. Stir it occasionally until melted and smooth. Line a Swiss roll tin with non-stick baking paper then pour in the melted chocolate, tilting the tin to level. Leave until set.

4 Once the chocolate is set, turn out on to a chopping board and carefully strip off the paper. Cut into 4 strips, the same length as the cooked sponge, using a large sharp knife that has been dipped into hot water.

5 Gently heat the apricot preserve and sieve to remove lumps. Brush over the top and sides of the cake. Carefully place the chocolate strips around the cake sides and press lightly. Leave to set for at least 10 minutes.

6 For the topping, whisk the cream to soft peaks and quickly fold into the melted chocolate with the brandy. Spoon the chocolate whipped cream into a pastry bag fitted with a star nozzle and pipe a decorative design of rosettes or shells over the surface. Dust with cocoa power and serve.

4

5

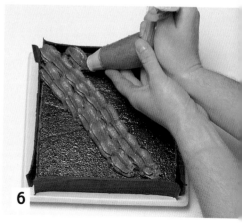
6

Valentine Heart Cupcakes

INGREDIENTS

Makes 12

150 g/5 oz butter, softened
150 g/5 oz caster sugar
3 medium eggs, beaten
1 tsp vanilla extract
2 tbsp milk
150 g/5 oz self-raising flour
½ tsp baking powder

To decorate:

225 g/8 oz ready-to-roll sugarpaste
pink and red paste food colouring
icing sugar, for dusting

For the cream cheese frosting:

50 g/2 oz unsalted butter, softened at
   room temperature
300 g/11 oz icing sugar, sifted
flavouring of choice
food colourings of choice
125 g/4 oz full-fat cream cheese

1 Preheat the oven to 180°C/350°F/Gas Mark 4, 10 minutes before baking and line a 12-hole muffin tray with deep paper cases.

2 Place the butter, sugar, eggs, vanilla extract and milk in a bowl, then sift in the flour and baking powder. Beat together for about 2 minutes with an electric hand mixer until pale and fluffy. Spoon into the paper cases and bake for 20–25 minutes until firm and golden. Cool on a wire rack.

3 To decorate, colour one third of the sugarpaste pink and one third red, leaving the rest white. Wrap a chopping board in clingfilm. Dust a clean, flat surface with icing sugar. Roll out the sugarpaste thinly and, using a cutter, cut out pink, red and white heart shapes, then leave to dry flat and harden for 2 hours (on the clingfilm-covered chopping board).

4 To make the cream cheese frosting, beat the butter and icing sugar together until light and fluffy. Add flavourings and colourings of choice and beat again. Add the cream cheese and whisk until light and fluffy. Do not over-beat, however, as the mixture can become runny. Place in a piping bag fitted with a star nozzle. Pipe a swirl on top of each cupcake and decorate with the hearts. Keep in a cool place for up to 2 days.

2

3

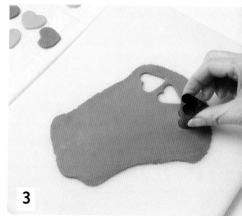

3

Easter Nest Cupcakes

INGREDIENTS

Makes 12

125 g/4 oz soft margarine
125 g/4 oz golden caster sugar
150 g/5 oz self-raising flour
2 tbsp cocoa powder
2 medium eggs
1 tbsp golden syrup

To decorate:

50 g/2 oz shredded wheat cereal
125 g/4 oz milk chocolate, broken
  into pieces
25 g/1 oz unsalted butter
chocolate mini eggs

For the buttercream:

150 g/5 oz unsalted butter,
  softened at room temperature
225 g/8 oz icing sugar, sifted
2 tbsp hot milk or water
1 tsp vanilla extract

1 Preheat the oven to 180°C/350°F/Gas Mark 4, 10 minutes before baking. Line a 12-hole bun tray with paper cases.

2 Place the margarine and the sugar in a large bowl, then sift in the flour and cocoa powder. In another bowl, beat the eggs with the syrup, then add to the first bowl. Whisk together with an electric beater for 2 minutes, or by hand with a wooden spoon until smooth.

3 Divide the mixture between the cases, filling them three-quarters full. Bake for about 15 minutes until they are springy to the touch in the centre. Turn out to cool on a wire rack.

4 Break up the shredded wheat finely. Melt the chocolate with the butter, then stir in the shredded wheat and let cool slightly. Line a plate with clingfilm. Mould the mixture into tiny nest shapes with your fingers, then place them on the lined plate. Freeze for a few minutes to harden.

5 To make the buttercream, beat the butter until light and fluffy, then beat in the sifted icing sugar and hot milk or water in two batches. Add the vanilla extract.

6 To decorate, swirl some buttercream over the top of each cupcake. Set a nest on top of each cupcake and fill with mini eggs. Keep for 2 days in a cool place in an airtight container.

2

4

6

Halloween Cobweb Cupcakes

INGREDIENTS

Makes 16–18

175 g/6 oz caster sugar
175 g/6 oz soft margarine
3 medium eggs, beaten
150 g/5 oz self-raising flour
1 tsp baking powder
25 g/1 oz cocoa powder

To decorate:
225 g/8 oz icing sugar, sifted
2 tbsp warm water
black and orange paste
  food colourings

1 Preheat the oven to 180°C/350°F/Gas Mark 4, 10 minutes before baking. Line two 12-hole bun trays with 16–18 paper or foil cases, depending on the depth of the holes.

2 Place the sugar, margarine and eggs in a bowl, then sift in the flour, baking powder and cocoa powder. Beat for 2 minutes or until smooth.

3 Spoon the mixture into the paper cases and bake for 15–20 minutes until well risen and the tops spring back when lightly pressed. Transfer to a wire rack to cool, then trim the tops of the cupcakes flat if they have any peaks.

4 To decorate the cupcakes, gradually mix the icing sugar with enough warm water to give a coating consistency. Colour a little of the icing black and place in a small paper icing bag. Colour the remaining icing bright orange.

5 Work on one cupcake at a time. Spread orange icing over the top of the cupcake. Snip a small hole in the end of the icing bag, then pipe a black spiral on top of the wet orange icing. Use a wooden toothpick and pull this through the icing to give a cobweb effect. Repeat with all the cupcakes and leave to set for 1 hour. Keep for 2 days in an airtight container in a cool place.

3

5

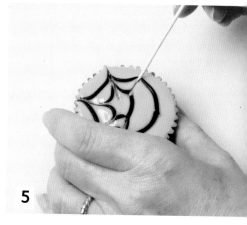

5

Wedding Cake

INGREDIENTS

Cuts into 50 slices

3 quantities Christmas Cake mixture
  (see page 20)
6 tbsp brandy or dark rum

To cover the cakes:

150 ml/10 tbsp sieved apricot
  jam, warmed
2.15 kg/4³/₄ lb almond paste (see
  page 46)
2.15 kg/4³/₄ lb ready-to-roll sugarpaste

To decorate:

450 g/1 lb ready-to roll sugarpaste
450 g/1 lb ready-made royal icing

1 Preheat the oven to 150°C/300°F/Gas Mark 2. Grease and treble line a 15 cm/6 inch, a 20 cm/8 inch and a 25.5 cm/10 inch round cake tin. Divide the mixture between the tins to the same depth. Bake for 1 hour, then reduce the oven to 140°C/275°F/Gas Mark 1 and bake respectively as follows: 1¹/₄ hours, 2 hours and 3 hours.

2 Brush each cake with brandy or rum, reserving 3 tablespoons, then with the jam. Divide the almond paste into three amounts weighing 350 g/12 oz, 800 g/1³/₄ lb and 1 kg/2¹/₄ lb. Roll out one third of the first amount into a disc the size of the top of the small cake and place on top. Roll out the remaining paste into a strip to cover the sides of the cake, then press on. Cover the remaining cakes and leave to dry out in a cool place for 2 days. Divide the sugarpaste as per the almond paste. On a surface dusted with icing sugar, roll out into circles large enough to cover the top and sides of each cake. Brush the remaining brandy or rum over the almond paste and place the sugarpaste on top. Smooth down over the cakes and trim the edges neatly. Stack the cakes.

3 Make 4 small roses for the top, 4 medium for the middle and 4 large for the base: mould a small cone of sugarpaste, then roll some into a pea-size ball, flatten out into a petal, then wrap this round the cone. Continue making and wrapping more petals, flute out the edges, then trim away the base and place the roses in an egg box to dry out and harden for 24 hours. Roll out the trimmings and cut out 4 small, 4 medium and 4 large leaves, mark on veins with a sharp knife, mould to curve and leave to dry. Place the royal icing in an icing bag fitted with a No. 0 plain nozzle and pipe sprig and dot decorations on each tier. Trim the base of each cake with a border of thinly rolled sugarpaste, then position the roses and leaves and stick in place with a dab of royal icing.

2

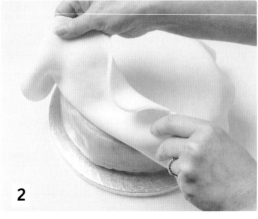
2

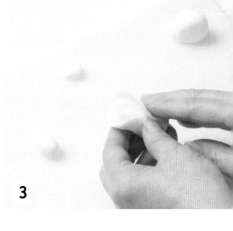
3

Birthday Numbers Cupcakes

INGREDIENTS

Makes 12–14

125 g/4 oz self-raising flour
125 g/4 oz caster sugar
125 g/4 oz soft margarine
2 medium eggs, beaten
1 tsp vanilla extract

To decorate:

225 g/8 oz ready-to-roll sugarpaste
paste food colourings
icing sugar, for dusting
1 batch buttercream
   (see page 32)
small candles
sprinkles and decorations

1 Preheat the oven to 180°C/350°F/Gas Mark 4, 10 minutes before baking. Line one or two 12-hole bun trays with 12–14 paper fairy-cake cases or silicone moulds, depending on the depth of the holes.

2 Sift the flour into a bowl and stir together with the caster sugar. Add the margarine, eggs and vanilla extract and beat together for about 2 minutes until smooth.

3 Spoon into the cases and bake in the preheated oven for 15–20 minutes until golden and firm to the touch. Turn out onto a wire rack. When cool, trim the tops flat if they have peaked slightly.

4 To decorate, colour batches of sugarpaste in bright colours. Dust a clean surface lightly with icing sugar. Thinly roll each colour of sugarpaste and cut out numbers using a set of cutters. Leave these for 2 hours to dry and harden.

5 Using a palette knife, spread the buttercream thickly onto the top of each cupcake. Place a small candle into each cupcake and stand the number up against this. Coat the edges of each cupcake with sprinkles and decorations. Serve within 8 hours as the numbers may start to soften.

4

5

5

Pirate Cupcakes

INGREDIENTS

Makes 14–16

125 g/4 oz self-raising flour
125 g/4 oz caster sugar
125 g/4 oz soft margarine
2 medium eggs, beaten
1 tsp vanilla extract

To decorate:

125 g/4 oz buttercream (see page 32)
450 g/1 lb ready-to-roll sugarpaste
pink, yellow, blue and black paste
   food colourings
small sweets and edible
   coloured balls
small tube red gel icing

1 Preheat the oven to 180°C/350°F/Gas Mark 4. Line two 12-hole bun trays with 14–16 paper fairy-cake cases or silicone moulds, depending on the depth of the holes.

2 Sift the flour into a bowl and stir together with the caster sugar. Add the margarine, eggs and vanilla extract and beat together for about 2 minutes until smooth.

3 Divide the mixture between the cases and bake in the preheated oven for 15–20 minutes until golden and firm to the touch. Turn out onto a wire rack. When cool, trim the tops flat if they have peaked slightly.

4 To decorate, lightly coat the top of each cupcake with a little buttercream. Colour the sugarpaste pale pink and roll out thinly on a surface dusted with icing sugar. Stamp out circles 6 cm/ 2½ inches wide and place these on the buttercream to cover the top of each cupcake.

5 Colour some scraps of sugarpaste blue, some yellow and a small amount black. Make triangular shapes from the blue and yellow icing and place these onto the pink icing at an angle to form hats. Stick coloured edible balls into the icing to decorate the hats. Make thin sausages from the black icing and press these across the cupcakes, then make tiny eye patches from black icing. Stick on a tiny sweet for each eye and pipe on red mouths with the gel icing. Keep for 2 days in an airtight container.

4

4

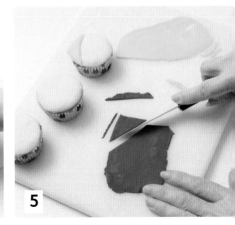

5

All-in-one Chocolate Fudge Cakes

INGREDIENTS

Makes 15

175 g/6 oz soft dark brown sugar
175 g/6 oz butter, softened
150 g/5 oz self-raising flour
25 g/1 oz cocoa powder
1/2 tsp baking powder
pinch salt
3 medium eggs, lightly beaten
1 tbsp golden syrup

For the fudge topping:

75 g/3 oz granulated sugar
150 ml/1/4 pint evaporated milk
175 g/6 oz dark chocolate,
  roughly chopped
40 g/1 1/2 oz unsalted butter, softened
125 g/4 oz soft fudge sweets, finely
  chopped

1 Preheat the oven to 180°C/350°F/Gas Mark 4, 10 minutes before baking. Oil and line a 28 x 18 x 2.5 cm/11 x 7 x 1 inch cake tin with nonstick baking parchment.

2 Place the soft brown sugar and butter in a bowl and sift in the flour, cocoa powder, baking powder and salt. Add the eggs and golden syrup, then beat with an electric whisk for 2 minutes before adding 2 tablespoons warm water and beating for a further 1 minute.

3 Turn the mixture into the prepared tin and level the top with the back of a spoon. Bake on the centre shelf of the preheated oven for 30 minutes, or until firm to the touch. Turn the cake out onto a wire rack and leave to cool before removing the baking parchment.

4 To make the topping, gently heat the sugar and evaporated milk in a saucepan, stirring frequently, until the sugar has dissolved. Bring the mixture to the boil and simmer for 6 minutes without stirring.

5 Remove the mixture from the heat. Add the chocolate and butter and stir until melted and blended. Pour into a bowl and chill in the refrigerator for 1–2 hours until thickened. Spread the topping over the cake, then sprinkle with the chopped fudge. Cut the cake into 15 squares before serving.

2

3

5

Butterfly Wings & Flowers Cupcakes

INGREDIENTS

Makes 12–14

150 g/5 oz butter, softened
150 g/5 oz caster sugar
175 g/5 oz self-raising flour
3 medium eggs, beaten
1 tsp lemon juice
2 tbsp milk

To decorate:

350 g/12 oz ready-to-roll sugarpaste
paste food colourings
icing sugar, for dusting
1 batch cream cheese frosting (see
    page 30)
gel icing tubes

1 Preheat the oven to 180°C/350°F/Gas Mark 4, 10 minutes before baking. Line one or two 12-hole muffin trays with 12–14 deep paper cases, depending on the depth of the holes.

2 Place the butter and sugar in a bowl, then sift in the flour. Add the beaten eggs to the bowl with the lemon juice and milk and beat until smooth. Spoon into the cases, filling them three-quarters full.

3 Bake in the preheated oven for about 18 minutes until firm to the touch in the centre. Turn out to cool on a wire rack.

4 To decorate, colour the sugarpaste in batches of lilac, blue, pink and yellow. Dust a clean, flat surface with icing sugar. Roll out the sugarpaste thinly and mark out daisy shapes and butterfly wings. Leave these to dry for 30 minutes until firm enough to handle.

5 Place the frosting in a piping bag fitted with a star nozzle and pipe swirls onto each cupcake. Press the wings and flowers onto the frosting and pipe on decorations with small gel icing tubes. Keep in an airtight container in a cool place for 3 days.

2

2

4

Football Cupcakes

INGREDIENTS

Makes 12–14

125 g/4 oz self-raising flour
125 g/4 oz caster sugar
125 g/4 oz soft margarine
2 medium eggs, beaten
1 tsp vanilla extract

For the apricot glaze:

225 g/8 oz apricot jam
1½ tbsp water
½ tsp lemon juice

For the almond paste:

125 g/4 oz sifted icing sugar
125 g/4 oz caster sugar
225 g/8 oz ground almonds
1 medium egg
1 tsp lemon juice

To decorate:

300 g/11 oz ready-to-roll sugarpaste
icing sugar, for dusting
black paste food colouring

1 Preheat the oven to 180°C/350°F/Gas Mark 4, 10 minutes before baking. Line two 12-hole bun trays with 12–14 paper fairy-cake cases or silicone moulds, depending on the depth of the holes. Sift the flour into a bowl and stir together with the caster sugar. Add the margarine, eggs and vanilla extract and beat together for about 2 minutes until smooth. Spoon into the cases and bake in the preheated oven for 15–20 minutes until golden and firm to the touch. Turn out onto a wire rack. When cool, trim the tops flat if they have peaked slightly.

2 To make the apricot glaze, place the jam, water and juice in a heavy-based saucepan and heat gently, stirring, until soft and melted. Boil rapidly for 1 minute, then press through a fine sieve with the back of a wooden spoon. Discard the pieces of fruit. To make the almond paste, Stir the sugars and ground almonds together in a bowl. Whisk the egg and lemon juice together and mix into the dry ingredients. Knead until the paste is smooth. Wrap tightly in clingfilm or foil to keep airtight and store in the refrigerator until needed. The paste can be made 2–3 days ahead of time but, after that, it will start to dry out and become difficult to handle. Knead on a surface lightly dusted with icing sugar until soft and pliable.

3 To decorate, lightly coat the top of each cake with a little apricot glaze. Roll out the almond paste on a surface dusted with icing sugar and cut out circles 6 cm/2½ inches wide and place these on the glaze to cover the top of each cake (you will have some left over). Colour half the sugarpaste black, and roll out all the sugarpaste. Using a small icing nozzle as a round guide, stamp out small white and black discs. Cut six straight edges away from each to form hexagons. Dampen the back of each hexagon with a little water, then stick the black discs between white ones, carefully matching up all the edges so they fit together. Keep for 3 days in an airtight container.

3

3

3

Step-by-Step, Practical Recipes Party Cakes: Tips & Hints

Helpful Hint

When making a show-stopping party cake it is a great idea to plan in advance how you wish it to be displayed; think about getting the right sized plate or platter, or even a decorative cake stand which matches the colour scheme of your party.

Helpful Hint

If you are making a cake in advance or wish to keep leftovers for another day, the best way to freeze it is to wrap it in two layers of clingfilm, add a layer of aluminium foil, place in a freezer bag and put in the freezer. To defrost the cake, set it out for several hours, and only remove the foil and clingfilm once the sponge has begun to soften to the touch.

Helpful Hint

To get the perfect cake mix you need to pay attention to the consistency of your butter. Always make sure it is very soft before you begin mixing; you should aim for it to have a consistency similar to mayonnaise. In order to achieve this, make sure you take the butter out of the fridge 60–90 minutes before you are likely to use it. Additionally, butter that has been sitting in the fridge for some time may have absorbed fridge odours which could taint the flavour of your cake. Instead it is recommended that you buy new any butter that you need.

Food Fact

If your cakes don't seem to be rising properly and you have ensured that all ingredient quantities were correct, it may be time to buy a new pot of baking powder. The effectiveness of this raising agent can decrease considerably if kept for long periods of time, a fresh pot may be just what you need!

Tasty Tip

Fresh eggs make the best cakes. Check how fresh yours are by placing them gently in a bowl of water. If they sink they are still fresh, but if they float it may be a good idea to consider buying some new ones.

Helpful Hint

If your cake recipe contains eggs, think about how they are to be used and plan ahead accordingly. Eggs separate best when they are cold, so at this stage in a recipe they should be taken from the fridge. However, egg whites whip best when warm so if this process is required allow the separated egg whites to reach room temperature first. If the recipe does not require eggs to be separated it is best to add them to your recipe at room temperature in order to avoid curdling; bring cool eggs to room temperature by placing them into a bowl of lukewarm water for 30 minutes.

Helpful Hint

To test if a cake is cooked through, open the oven close to the final cooking time, pull the rack out a little and gently insert a clean skewer into the centre of the cake. If the skewer comes out clean then the cake is ready and you can remove it from the oven completely. You should also check that the sponge feels the same firmness at the centre of the cake as at the edges when you press gently with your fingertips.

Helpful Hint

It is important that you let the oven reach the necessary temperature before you put your cake in; if you put it in too soon, the mixture will not rise correctly. Additionally, do not allow your finished cake mixture to stand around too long before you put it in the preheated oven as the raising agent will be activated as soon as it is combined with the mixture's wet ingredients.

Helpful Hint

Always keep the oven door closed until you know that your cake is approaching its final cooking time. No matter how tempting it may be to open it beforehand and take a peek, the rush of cold air from the open door may cause the cake to collapse. Aside from sticking to final cooking times, a good sign of a cake being almost ready is when its delicious smell starts to fill the kitchen.

Helpful Hint

Why not make extra cake mix and bake some cupcakes with it – that way you are creating an extra option for food at the party without using extra time in preparation. Genius!

First published in 2013 by
FLAME TREE PUBLISHING LTD
Crabtree Hall, Crabtree Lane, Fulham,
London, SW6 6TY, United Kingdom
www.flametreepublishing.com

The CIP record for this book is available from the British Library • Printed in China

NOTE: Recipes using uncooked eggs should be avoided by infants, the elderly, pregnant women and anyone suffering from an illness.

18 17 16 15 14 13   10 9 8 7 6 5 4 3 2 1

ISBN: 978-0-85775-852-1

ACKNOWLEDGEMENTS: Authors: Catherine Atkinson, Juliet Barker, Ann Nicol, Gina Steer, Vicki Smallwood, Carol Tennant, Mari Mererid Williams, Elizabeth Wolf-Cohen and Simone Wright. Photography: Colin Bowling, Paul Forrester and Stephen Brayne. Home Economists and Stylists: Jacqueline Bellefontaine, Mandy Phipps, Vicki Smallwood and Penny Stephens. Some props supplied by Barbara Stewart at Surfaces. Publisher and Creative Director: Nick Wells. Editorial: Catherine Taylor, Laura Bulbeck, Esme Chapman, Emma Chafer. Design and Production: Chris Herbert, Mike Spender and Helen Wall.